MARKETING YOUR INVENTION

THIRD EDITION

ABA Section of Intellectual Property Law

ABA
Defending Liberty
Pursuing Justice

Printed in the United States of America

13 12 11 10 09   5 4 3 2 1

**Cataloging-in-Publication Data is on file
with the Library of Congress.**

Marketing Your Invention, 3e
Section of Intellectual Property Law
ISBN: 978-1-60442-365-5

Discounts are available for books ordered in bulk. Special consideration is given to state bars, CLE programs, and other bar-related organizations. Inquire at Book Publishing, ABA Publishing, American Bar Association, 321 North Clark Street, Chicago, Illinois 60654-7598.

www.ababooks.org

Table of Contents

Acknowledgments for the First Edition

The editor wishes to acknowledge the contributions of the following individuals who have worked on this project:

Burton P. Beatty
Keith Bergmann
Adrian T. Calderone
Roger Norman Coe
John L. Gray
Mark C. Jacobs
Charles G. Lamb
Donald W. Margolis
Leonard B. Mackey

James C. McLaughlin
Dennis M. McWilliams
Peter C. Michalos
Joseph P. Atigon
Steven P. Shurtz
Eugene S. Stephens
William M. Yates
John L. Young

also Michele A. Bridges, ABA-IPL Staff Director; Dennis J. Helms, for his able editorial assistance; and especially Clinton S. Janes, Jr., former Chair of ABA-IPL Committee 106 (Inventors); and John R. Kirk, Jr., present Chair of ABA-IPL Committee 106. Lastly, special thanks to Joyce Ross, Law Office Administrator, for organizing, typing, and checking this material. Without your contributions, this booklet would not have been possible.

Richard C. Woodbridge, Editor

ACKNOWLEDGMENTS FOR THE SECOND EDITION

The editor of the second edition wishes to acknowledge first the contributions of the Internet, as well the following individuals:

Rel S. Ambrozy	William B. Gowanlock
Brian R. Balow	Lynn P. Hendrix
Erwin J. Basinski	Brian J. McNamara
Robert S. Bramson	Linda S. Resh
Peter S. Canelias	Jerald E. Rosenblum

Special thanks to John G. Posa, patent attorney, inventor and artist, for contributing the artwork for the cover.

Maria Comninou

Acknowledgments for the Third Edition

The editor of the third edition wishes to acknowledge the following individuals:

David Lowry
Peter D. McDermott
John P. Iwanicki
Dale A. Malone

Mark Dickson, Editor

FOREWORD TO THE FIRST EDITION

The object of this booklet is to supply the independent inventor or small corporate entrepreneur with practical guidelines for marketing an invention. It is not intended to be an exhaustive study of the subject matter but, rather, is designed to present general information in an effort to help move an invention into the marketplace. Emphasis is placed upon understanding the role patents play in promoting, licensing, and selling an invention. This is not a "do-it-yourself" manual, but is offered to stimulate thinking and provide suggestions along practical, not theoretical lines. A patent attorney should be consulted in advance to insure compliance with existing laws and to avoid unexpected pitfalls.

FOREWORD TO THE SECOND EDITION

In the ten years since the first edition, many spectacular changes have occurred in the world of Intellectual Property, including changes in U.S. Patent law, the 6 millionth patent, Intellectual Property globalization, and some harmonization through international agreements, the Internet, and vigorous trade and inventive activities worldwide. Nevertheless, the basic advice provided in this booklet has remained sound, and the task of the second editor was mainly to update the law, including the change in the patent term, the creation of the provisional application, the patentability of computer programs and business methods, and to direct the inventor to the vast array of additional resources on the Internet.

FOREWORD TO THE THIRD EDITION

In today's economic world, it is hard to overestimate the value of intellectual property. In the face of ever-changing technology, protection of that intellectual property has become an essential part of every business plan for moving forward toward the future. In this updated booklet, we continue to provide basic information for independent inventors and small corporate entrepreneurs for protecting their inventions and getting them into the marketplace. The materials and advice collected here are not meant to be exhaustive but merely a first tangible starting point down the long path toward successful commercialization.

*The journey to successful commercialization of an invention is one
of many steps and involves many people. Typically the steps occur in
the following order.*

PATENTS

At the outset, the entrepreneur/inventor should discuss his or her idea with
a registered patent attorney. During the initial office interview, the patent
attorney will probably talk about the legal requirements for patentability.
Patents are issued by the federal government, and the criteria for obtaining
a patent are set forth in Title 35 of the United States Code. A number of
pamphlets are available as a guide on this subject. The inventor may wish
to visit online or write to the United States Patent and Trademark Office,
the American Bar Association, or the American Intellectual Property Law
Association for useful publications. Their websites, addresses, and the names
of some publications are listed in Appendix A.

A new invention need not be as revolutionary as Thomas Edison's
light bulb in order to be patentable. A broad range of products and pro-
cesses are patentable. The most common reasons that an invention is not
patentable are:

- It falls into an unpatentable category, e.g., laws of nature or abstract
  ideas. Computer programs and business method inventions have long
  been patentable so long as they lead to a useful and concrete result
  which satisfies the other requirements of patentability.
- It has been invented by another who has not abandoned or suppressed
  the idea.
- It has been in public use, the subject of public knowledge, or on sale
  for more than one (1) year before a U.S. patent application has been
  filed.
- It is "obvious" (to one of ordinary skill in the relevant field) in view of
  prior public use or knowledge. Prior public knowledge includes, for
  example, earlier patents and publications.

There are some complexities to these reasons why an invention may not
be patentable, and a patent attorney can provide additional explanation.
Other important considerations may also affect the ability to obtain patent
protection.

There must be full disclosure to the patent attorney. Failure to provide full disclosure may undermine the accuracy and reliability of the patent attorney's advice and the validity of the patent. Since all communications between the inventor and his or her patent attorney are considered to be confidential and protected by the "attorney/client privilege," it is to the inventor's benefit to discuss thoroughly all aspects of the invention at the first interview.

The inventor should prepare a written disclosure of the idea when it is conceived (i.e., when it is first invented) or as soon as possible. The ability to prove the date of invention sometimes becomes critical to obtaining a patent. Therefore, it is highly recommended that the written disclosure be signed and dated on each page by the inventor and also be witnessed by at least one, and preferably two, disinterested witnesses on each page. Be aware that, where an invention has multiple inventors, a co-inventor does not qualify as a disinterested witness. The witnesses should sign and date each page under the caption, "Read and Understood." The disclosure should be legible and in ink. It does not have to be typed if the inventor's handwriting is legible. It must, however, be understandable. A couple of good ink sketches and a few handwritten pages are frequently sufficient. A good disclosure should include:

1. A written description of the preferred embodiment, that is, a description of the version or example of the invention that the inventor at that time considers to be the best. This is referred to in the patent law as the "best mode." The description should include enough details of the invention and an explanation of its operation so that one of ordinary skill in that field of technology can make and use the invention without undue experimentation;
2. A sufficient number of sketches so that one familiar with the technology can readily understand what the invention is;
3. A brief description and sketches of likely alternative embodiments of the invention;
4. A statement of the advantages to be gained from the invention's use; and
5. A list of all co-inventors.

After the invention has been discussed with the patent attorney, a patent search may be recommended to identify any prior patents that disclose the same or similar concepts. Reviewing the search results, that is, the so-called prior art identified by the search, with the advice of the patent attorney can help the inventor make an informed decision whether to undertake the effort and cost of preparing and prosecuting a patent application. A typical patent search includes a review of all of the relevant patents on file in the United States Patent and Trademark Office (PTO) in Alexandria, Virginia. While these prior art searches were done by hand in earlier times, they now most often are performed as an electronic search in one of the databases maintained by the PTO. A prior art search may also include a review of articles, books, and other publications which are relevant to the invention. Many of these texts can be accessed by computer or searched through the facilities of major libraries.

The inventor may wish to search and review some of the prior art before commencing a professional patent search. Many states have libraries that include a collection of patents and provide (for a fee) access to complete PTO electronic databases. Those libraries are listed in Appendix B. In addition, free electronic searches are available on the Internet (including the PTO's website and private sites such as Google), although they do not cover the earlier patents. If the inventor is close to the U.S. Patent and Trademark Office in Alexandria, Virginia, the inventor could do the searching there, because the patents at the U.S. Patent and Trademark Office are physically organized and accessible by field of technology according to class and subclass. The inventor should pass the results of any preliminary patent search on to his patent attorney to help inform the decision whether to have a search performed by a professional patent searcher.

If the results of the professional patent search are encouraging (i.e., the prior art located by the search indicates that patent protection is probably available), then preparing a patent application is the next step. The cost of preparing a patent application can be significant and should be discussed with the patent attorney in advance. Most patent applications, especially those having mechanical or electrical features, will require special patent drawings. The drawings are almost always prepared by a qualified patent illustrator. Once the application is complete to the satisfaction of the patent attorney and the inventor, the attorney will file it in the United States Patent and Trademark Office along with the U.S. Government filing fee, the drawings, a prior art statement (if indicated), a Small Business Entity form (if indicated), a declaration (or oath) form, a power of attorney form, an assignment form (if desired), and occasionally other documents. Standard forms can be downloaded free of charge from the PTO website. Almost all of these materials may now be filed electronically by the patent attorney.

The typical patent application takes more than two years to work its way through the Patent and Trademark Office before it becomes an issued patent (a period termed "prosecution of an application" during which goods under the claimed invention can be designated as "patent pending"). Between six and twelve months, and often more, may elapse before the applicant receives a "First Office Action"—a communication from the Patent and Trademark Office with its comments about the patentability of the claimed invention. An accelerated examination procedure, with special requirements, is also available.

During the pendency of an application there may be several office actions that will have to be responded to in writing by the patent attorney. Therefore, there will be ongoing interactions between the inventor and the patent attorney as well as ongoing expenses depending upon the complexity of the prosecution. If the patent application is allowed, the U.S. Government also charges an issue fee that must be paid before the patent is permitted to issue. In rare cases, the application might also be the subject of an interference proceeding if another party invents and applies for a patent on approximately the same thing at the same time.

Instead of filing a regular patent application, the inventor has the option of filing a provisional patent application (PPA) with a lower initial filing fee. The PPA establishes the filing date and confers "patent pending" status on the invention. It gives the inventor one year to do market research and decide whether to pursue the invention. During that year the inventor must file a regular (non-provisional) patent application, because the PPA automatically becomes abandoned after one year and the filing date is lost unless a regular application is filed within that period.

The PPA is not examined and does not require the inclusion of claims, but it must provide sufficient disclosure to support the later-filed non-provisional application, otherwise the PPA priority date will be lost. For this reason, it is recommended that the services of a patent attorney are used in preparing and filing the PPA. The requirements and additional information for filing a PPA can be found at the PTO website, from which a standard cover sheet and other forms can be downloaded.

Although the bulk of all First Office Actions are some form of rejection, 60–70 percent of all patent applications eventually result in issued patents.

The term of a typical U.S. Utility Patent is twenty (20) years from its filing date, but the term can be adjusted to compensate for delays that are not the fault of the applicant. Legislation enacted on November 19, 1999 guarantees the diligent patent applicant a term of seventeen (17) years for applications filed on or after six months from the enactment date. There are fees due at the time an application issues as a patent; in addition, renewal charges, known as maintenance fees, must be paid three and one-half, seven and one-half, and eleven and one-half years after the date of issuance in order to keep the patent in force.

Evaluating the Potential of New Technology

The evaluation of an invention is an inherently speculative process. As a first suggestion, the entrepreneur should talk to other inventors who have been successful in the same or similar fields. There is no substitute for talking with an individual who has been there before. A wealth of information is now available on the Internet from various inventor-run organizations. The names and Internet addresses of a representative sample of these organizations are given in Appendix C.

Invention evaluation services can also be helpful. Many of those organizations are associated with academic institutions. Their charges and depth of analysis vary broadly. However, the inventor should beware of for-profit organizations that offer "invention marketing" services. Often, such companies charge large, up-front fees in exchange for the promise to assist the inventor in obtaining a patent and marketing the invention. In many cases, however, the companies seek to obtain only a design patent (which is faster and cheaper to prosecute but provides a scope of protection quite different from a utility patent) and make only token efforts to market the invention. The inventor considering such an arrangement is well advised to review the terms of the contract with an attorney in order to fully understand what the company is (and is not) promising to do. It is also a good idea to ask for, and check, references to see what the company has done for other inventors.

Several factors relating to a new process or product ought to be considered as they are applicable to all inventions:

(a) Does the invention actually work as anticipated? Is the technology feasible?

(b) Is there a market for the product? An estimate of the potential size of the market for the invention must be undertaken at some point. As part of the process a market survey may be necessary to assess the good and bad points of the product. The market survey may also take into account price sensitivity and, accordingly, the entrepreneur should have a good idea of the cost of manufacture before undertaking a market survey. If the market is not already established, the market survey may have to estimate the size of the advertising budget that will be necessary to attract buyers to the new product.

   (c) What is the cost of manufacturing the product? An estimate should be made to determine the necessary investment for making the new product or carrying out the new process or, alternatively, for making modifications to existing production facilities.

   (d) Do the people who plan to make and sell the product or process have the necessary business and financial experience?

   (e) Is the product or process patented? If not already patented, careful consideration should be given to obtaining an expert opinion on the patentability of the invention and, if affirmative, to having a patent application promptly filed and prosecuted. As already noted, most of the government fees for filing and prosecuting a regular application may be deferred for up to one year by filing a provisional patent application.

   (f) Is the product or process the subject of a patent owned by another party? If so, the dominant patent of the other party might limit the rights of the entrepreneur.

In summary, all of the above factors must be weighed in predicting the likely profitability of an invention. If the results of the foregoing analysis are encouraging, then the information will probably be incorporated into a business plan. A comprehensive evaluation of the potential of a new product or process must be conducted in order to arrive at a reasonable estimate of the value of the invention.

Timing is another factor that may have a significant effect on the value of an invention. For example, the life of a typical utility patent is twenty (20) years from the filing date, after which the invention can be freely exploited by anyone. A variety of production and/or management factors, however, may shift the period of commercial importance enjoyed by an invention to a time earlier or later than the period of patent protection. To illustrate, the marketing period for a toy is often short-lived and may have passed even before a patent is granted. In order to extend the life cycle of a particular invention, an improvement made on the basic invention should be promptly evaluated for its patentability and, if possible, consideration given to filing a new patent application or PPA covering the improvement. Be sure to involve the patent attorney well before the improvement is commercialized or disclosed to the public.

It is common for inventors to underestimate the cost and difficulty of commercializing their inventions and to overestimate the market size and the likelihood of consumer acceptance. As a gross generalization, inventors typically underestimate their costs by a factor of 2 and their time to full commercialization by a factor of 3. Inventors must be prepared to face and surmount difficulties and frustration before an invention returns a profit.

Drafting a Business Plan

A well-written business plan is important for two reasons. First, it will help the entrepreneur organize his or her endeavor efficiently. Second, most serious investors will not finance an entrepreneur without a good business plan.

There are several good sources of help for the entrepreneur who wishes to draft a business plan. Certified public accountants are especially helpful because they are good at assembling the financial information that goes into the business plan. Many of the large national CPA firms have special groups that assist entrepreneurs with high technology in the development of their business plan. Several major accounting firms also produce excellent booklets, which they distribute for free, on the preparation of business plans. Those booklets include checklists indicating essential elements.

Free business counseling is available from volunteer and retired business executives in non-profit groups like SCORE, with templates, programs, and advice available through the Internet. The business departments of community colleges and certain state and private universities are also a good source for business planning assistance. For example, the Rutgers University Technical Assistance Program (RUTAP) assists entrepreneurs by providing one-on-one counseling to help in the formulation and development of business plans. In addition, RUTAP presents a monthly New Jersey Entrepreneurs Forum during which the entrepreneur can present his idea for review by a panel of experienced reviewers. Similar programs exist in other states.

There are a number of individuals who hold themselves out as management and business consultants. Management consultants tend to be more expensive than other types of advisers, but their expertise is frequently worth the additional cost.

There are many companies currently dedicated to providing business-planning services and certain large firms have special departments devoted to such services. Regardless of whom you choose as an assistant in drafting your business plan, make sure that you shop around until you find an individual with solid experience and good references.

Going into Business for Yourself

The three most common forms of legal business structure are defined as follows:

(a) *Sole proprietorship*—is the simplest form of doing business. No special steps have to be taken to be treated as a sole proprietorship. Many states, however, require that the name of the business be registered with the county or the state where business is conducted, particularly if its name is not that of its proprietor and, of course, the sole proprietor is responsible for all taxes including local, county, state, and federal. In a sole proprietorship the individual is liable for all debts of the business activity and is entitled to all net profits therefrom. Many small "mom and pop" businesses, such as grocery stores, are sole proprietorships.

(b) *Partnership*—is when more than one person is involved. Most partnerships are formed by a written agreement between the parties; however, a partnership may be implied by law in many states without a written agreement. Partnerships are either general or limited. In a general partnership all of the partners share in the profits according to their percentage of capital contribution and liabilities without limitation. In a limited partnership, the limited partners are generally liable only to the extent of their agreed-upon capital contributions.

(c) *Corporation*—a corporation is formed by filing a Certificate of Incorporation with the Secretary of State of one of the 50 states or the District of Columbia. It has the advantage of providing limited liability to the shareholders of the corporation. The corporate form of business also lends itself to investment because shares of the corporation can be sold to outside investors. Regular corporations are "C" corporations for tax purposes but shareholders can elect to be treated by the IRS as "S" corporations and thereby resemble a partnership for tax, but not liability, purposes. Many states have their own form of limited liability corporation, which may or may not be well-suited to an inventor's circumstances.

An entrepreneur should consult with an attorney familiar with the corporate laws in his state. As a general rule of thumb, it is advisable to "incorporate at home" rather than to incorporate in another state. There may be special circumstances, however, where incorporation in a foreign state, such as Delaware, might be warranted.

In addition, it is advisable to discuss a potential incorporation with a CPA prior to completing the formalities. Often the personal financial situation of the entrepreneur or the investors may dictate the form of the business vehicle. For example, if the entrepreneur decides to incorporate, should the corporation be a "C" or an "S" type? Such decisions are relatively simple to carry out, but can be very difficult to undo later if the initial decision proves to be disadvantageous. Also, a CPA can help set up the books and may be in a position to file some of the forms with the Federal Government thereby relieving the incorporating attorney of such responsibility.

If the entrepreneur intends to raise money through public or private placement of securities, then he or she should make sure that the attorney is familiar with the state's Blue Sky laws as well as federal securities regulations. State Blue Sky laws control the issuance of securities within a state and are frequently more restrictive than federal securities regulations. It is easy to make a mistake in this area and the consequences of a mistake are severe. Therefore, analyze these matters with an attorney at an early stage of the venture.

Before a sophisticated investor puts money into a new enterprise, he or she will frequently perform a "due diligence" review of the legal and business history of the enterprise and the entrepreneur. Due diligence reviews are also performed by underwriters who may sell the securities to the public. A poorly structured partnership or corporation may kill a public issuance of securities at an early stage for failure to pass through the due diligence review phase. Therefore, the entrepreneur should not attempt to cut corners when organizing the business venture if there are any serious plans to sell securities to the public.

Employment Agreements

All entrepreneurs should review their employment agreements with prior employers to determine whether there are restrictive covenants limiting their activities. Also, if the invention was made at a time when the inventor was employed under a contract that assigned inventions to the employer, an attorney should be consulted to help confirm ownership of the invention. Some employers may limit the ability of employees to work for competitors, and the use of confidential information learned as an employee is usually restricted. Many bitter lawsuits have been waged between employers and their former employees based on issues arising out of employment agreements. Those agreements should be reviewed by an attorney early on to determine if there are any substantial limitations on the activities of the entrepreneur.

Similarly, an entrepreneur should have employment agreements with all corporate officers and employees which include an assignment of intellectual property rights to the new corporation and reasonable restrictions on the post-employment activities of terminated officers and employees. Care should be taken to avoid overly broad restrictions, which are disfavored by courts. Again, the attorney can assist in crafting restrictions that protect the interests of the entrepreneur's business but are still likely to be upheld by a reviewing court.

Confidential Disclosure Agreements

It is often necessary for the entrepreneur to show his technology to a third party, such as a potential investor, a manufacturer, a supplier, or other entity in the chain of commerce. Of course, an effort should be made to obtain patent, trademark, or copyright protection (as evidenced by at least a filed application) before such a disclosure is made. Even if patent, trademark, or copyright protection has already been obtained, it is generally desirable to have the third party sign a "confidential disclosure agreement," a written agreement in which the third party agrees to keep the information confidential. It is advisable that the enterprise develops its own standardized confidential disclosure form that it can use to protect itself when it submits the information to a third party.

Manufacturing and Distributing Alternatives

There are basically four modes by which an entrepreneur can manufacture and distribute his or her invention:

(a) The entrepreneur can be the manufacturer and distributor of the product. This is the most difficult approach, but the one with the highest potential reward.

(b) The entrepreneur can be the distributor of the product, but have a third party manufacture it. This is sometimes referred to as contract-manufacture or an OEM (Original Equipment Manufacturer) arrangement. Distribution can be carried out by traditional methods, or online.

(c) The entrepreneur can manufacture the invention and have someone else distribute the product. For example, the product might be distributed by the manufacturers' representatives, by mail order or catalogue, online, or through a chain of stores. This mode lends itself best to situations where the product is relatively easy for the entrepreneur to manufacture but difficult to distribute.

(d) The entrepreneur can engage a third party to manufacture and distribute the product. This is the typical licensing situation in which the rights to manufacture and sell the product have been transferred to a third party by the entrepreneur in return for license fees. The advantage of this mode of operation is that the entrepreneur has to put only the minimal amount of effort into the enterprise. Finding a licensee who is ready, willing, and able to manufacture and sell the product at a high royalty rate, however, can often be a difficult proposition.

The rise of the Internet opens up many more opportunities for self-distribution than were previously available to entrepreneurs. Potential manufacturers, even across the world, can be identified with a simple search. Expanded geographic markets for an invention are also available, especially where the product is relatively easy to ship. Internet search engines and on-line auctions like eBay make it easier than ever for an entrepreneur to be found by target customers.

Licensing Inventions

The first step in licensing an invention is to identify potential licensees. Most public libraries include indices of manufacturing companies broken down according to industry and size, among other characteristics. One of the most commonly used indices is the Thomas Register, currently available on the Internet. Other sources are also listed in Appendix D.

The next step is to communicate with potential licensees. Most large companies, and many smaller ones, will not evaluate outside submissions of new technology unless the submitter first signs the company's disclosure form. Company-prepared idea submission forms are drafted to protect the company. Because large companies routinely receive hundreds, if not thousands of good unsolicited ideas annually, it is necessary for them to have pre-signed disclosure agreements to avoid internal and external conflicts. Many companies will not agree to review new technology in confidence. Accordingly, the entrepreneur should take steps to protect his technology through patents, trademarks, or copyrights prior to attempting to submit the new technology to a company. Upon completion of the disclosure form by the entrepreneur, the company may agree to evaluate the invention, but generally will agree to do no more than report its interest or lack thereof to the submitter.

The idea submission to the evaluating organization should be signed, dated, and witnessed. A conformed copy should be retained by the entrepreneur. The description should be as detailed as possible so that the invention can be properly and thoroughly evaluated. Because many companies are reluctant to examine outside inventions, a sketchy or incomplete description may result in a summary rejection of the invention.

Most large companies receive hundreds of unsolicited submissions each year. Really big companies, especially the automobile and toy manufacturers, receive thousands of unsolicited submissions per year. Consequently, most companies can only use one or two percent of the ideas submitted to them. The entrepreneur should realize that the chance of getting a large company to license new technology is relatively small. Most companies are not ready, willing, or able to commit the manpower and money to more than one or two new technologies at a time. Some companies prefer only technology developed in-house and this is often referred to as the "NIH (Not Invented Here) Syndrome."

A license can be limited to a single party (exclusive) or can be granted to several parties (nonexclusive). Other important aspects of licensing include foreign rights, trade secrets, know-how, and royalty payments, and the right (or duty) to sue third-party infringers. With respect to royalty payments, licenses may provide for a single lump-sum payment, or a royalty of a specified amount for each product produced under the license, or a royalty in the form of a percentage of the receipts from the sale of the licensed subject matter.

The inventor should be aware that there is no "standard" royalty rate. In some industries, such as the automotive, the royalty rate can be as low as 1 percent or less and, in other industries, such as the pharmaceutical industry, royalty rates can be as high as 20 percent or more. Average royalty rates tend to run around 5 percent of "net sales," but royalty rates can vary widely depending upon the nature of the license (exclusive versus nonexclusive), potential sales, and the risks taken by the licensee, and other factors.

The inventor should also be aware of the difficulty of getting out of a license agreement if the manufacturing or sales program is not going smoothly. Many license agreements include a minimum royalty provision that requires the licensee to pay the licensor a minimum royalty each year or the licensee will lose the license. All good license agreements should include some kind of escape provision if the licensee does not do an acceptable job of selling the product.

The major attraction of a license is that it can provide the entrepreneur (licensor) with income at a much lower level of risk and commitment than if the inventor were to personally seek to exploit his invention. A license may also be advantageous in permitting the inventor to enter domestic and foreign markets which otherwise might not have been open to him because of trade restrictions, quotas, taxes, or freight considerations.

License negotiation and drafting can be very complex and are, therefore, beyond the scope of this booklet. There is no "standard license" to fit all situations. Efforts at licensing should be commenced only with expert assistance from an experienced patent attorney or an attorney with substantial experience in licensing technology.

Many companies prefer to buy an invention outright in order to assume total control of the technology and thereby avoid the need for further accounting to the entrepreneur. An entrepreneur typically sells his invention by an "assignment" of his entire right, title, and interest to the invention including any patent applications or issued patents. More recently, patent holding companies have emerged. Such companies amass collections of patents, usually in related technologies, in order to license them to manufacturers. These companies typically have more capital than an individual inventor can raise and, thus, enjoy greater leverage in license negotiations. Such companies also have the resources to undertake patent litigation if necessary to enforce the patent. Patents may also be assigned by private sale, including auctions. At any given time, a significant number of patents are listed for sale on eBay, and there are a number of specialty brokers and auctioneers who deal in patents and other intellectual property.

Marketing Representatives

One technique for selling new products is to employ a marketing representative. A marketing representative is compensated on the basis of a commission for each item sold. The commission is typically a percentage of the price of the product. Marketing representatives can be located from databases found at larger public libraries and on the Internet. The advantage of using marketing representatives is that they do not cost the inventor anything for the services provided. On the negative side, marketing representatives tend to promote those products that sell the best. If the product does not sell well, the marketing representative may lose interest in it.

Inventor Organizations

There are numerous inventor organizations on the national, regional, and local levels that act as support groups. Their basic functions are to lend encouragement and provide education to inventors. A tabulation of representative organizations is provided in Appendix C and more comprehensive listings are available on the Internet. Although not strictly inventor organizations, the U.S. Patent and Trademark Office, the American Bar Association, and the American Intellectual Property Law Association will provide literature and information to inventors upon request (see Appendix A).

Invention Promotion Firms

A large number of organizations allege that they can provide significant assistance to inventors. It is unfortunate that many promise much more than they can deliver. They are often known as invention brokers and their names and telephone numbers can be found in the classified sections of popular magazines, and advertised on television, radio, and the Internet. It is prudent for the entrepreneur to be skeptical of such organizations, especially if the invention broker requires a substantial up-front payment. Before committing to work with such an organization, the entrepreneur should first ascertain how successful the organization has been in promoting inventors and selling technology. Some important questions to ask are: How many of their clients have made more money than they have paid into the organization? Do they have a list of satisfied customers whom they can supply as references? Have they been investigated recently by legal authorities? What sort of rating do they have with the Better Business Bureau? How long have they been in business? Have they been in business under previous names?

Invention brokers make large sums of money off of gullible inventors. The entrepreneur should check with a knowledgeable patent attorney before approaching any invention broker. The experience of most inventors with invention brokers is that the inventors lose money in the long run. The Federal Trade Commission has investigated and brought fraud charges against several invention promotion firms in the past. Details of the investigations undertaken by the FTC as part of "Project Mousetrap" are still available at the FTC website.

To foster integrity in invention promotion services, Congress enacted legislation requiring invention promoters to disclose in writing materially relevant information before entering into a contract with an inventor. In addition, the legislation establishes a federal cause of action for inventors who are injured by fraudulent statements, omissions, and misrepresentations, and requires the PTO to publicize complaints involving invention promoters (http://www.uspto.gov/web/offices/com/iip/complaints.htm).

Sources of Financing

The most common sources of financing for start-ups are relatives and friends. This is especially true if the amount involved is relatively small, i.e., a quarter of a million dollars or less. Therefore, the entrepreneur should first look close to home if the financial needs of the start-up are relatively modest.

Banks can provide start-up funds but they usually require the entrepreneur to provide collateral and to personally guarantee the loan. Many banks will consider financing a new business if the loans are backed by the Small Business Administration. The more prudent entrepreneur should make contact with the Small Business Administration before approaching a bank concerning a loan. Some banks, particularly smaller regional banks, work actively with the Small Business Administration to assist start-up businesses in their market areas.

Some entrepreneurs think of approaching conventional venture capital firms before they approach any other source. Unfortunately, the competition for venture capital money is intense and most conventional venture capital firms receive literally hundreds of submissions a year. The venture capital funding process has become more sophisticated in recent times and entrepreneurs are expected to put forth well-thought-out business plans and evidence of intellectual property protection as part of their funding requests. Online services are available to assist entrepreneurs in preparing proposals and locating venture capital groups and other "angel investors" that may provide sources of seed capital. Entrepreneurs are advised to speak with an attorney before signing any venture capital agreement since venture capital groups often require a substantial equity position in any new company and other concessions in exchange for funding.

Small Business Investment Companies (SBICs) are a special type of venture organization generally directed towards small business investments. They are especially attractive for start-ups. SBICs are licensed by the Small Business Administration and part of their funding comes from federal funds. To locate an SBIC in your vicinity, visit the Small Business Administration website, or call or write to the National Association of Small Business Investment Companies, both listed in Appendix E.

More and more states are becoming active in the area of financing high-technology start-ups. For example, the Ben Franklin Technology Partners in Pennsylvania has provided seed capital in the form of innovation investment and enterprise-growth grants for over two decades. Similar programs exist in many states with recognized high tech development centers such as California, Massachusetts, Oregon, and Texas.

The Small Business Innovation Research program (SBIR) is administered by 11 federal agencies which must set aside a certain proportion of their research and development funds for individuals and independently owned companies with 500 or fewer employees. Therefore, the funding provided by the SBIR program must fit within the needs of the R & D objectives of the participating federal agencies. Grants are provided to successful applicants in three phases. More information, including the list participating agencies, can be obtained from the U.S. Small Business Administration Office of Technology, 1409 Third Street, SW Washington, D.C. 20416; telephone (202) 205-6450, or from the SBIR's website.

Professionals are frequently a good source of leads to individuals capable of providing financing. Lawyers and accountants are especially useful sources of information because they come into contact with individuals with substantial means. Most major U.S. accounting firms and large law firms have made a special effort to assist budding high-tech start-ups.

If the inventor is not successful in finding financing from the conventional sources of capital, other sources worth investigating include venture capital networks, small business incubators, and county and community development funds. Appendix E lists some sources of financing that the entrepreneur may consider.

Naming the Product and the Company

It is a common misconception that the filing and acceptance of a Certificate of Incorporation by a state automatically permits the company to use the name in the charter without legal challenges from third parties. First of all, the mere acceptance of a charter by a Secretary of State does not protect the company against individuals and organizations who have prior rights to the name of the corporation whether as a business name or a trademark. Second, incorporation in one state does not permit the company to use its company name in any of the other 49 states. In fact, it is theoretically possible for 50 different companies to incorporate under the same name in each of the 50 different states! Therefore, it is advisable, especially if there is to be any significant amount of interstate commerce, to check the availability of a company name before it is registered with the Secretary of State of the state of incorporation. Many states have official websites where corporate names can be searched. Even so, a corporate name clearance search should be performed by an experienced patent and trademark attorney before a name is finally selected and used.

Similarly, the name of a product or service (i.e., trademark) should be searched and cleared before it is used. There are over 2,000,000 federal trademarks registered with the U.S. Patent and Trademark Office and only about 25,000 words in the typical English vocabulary. Therefore, the chances of duplication and confusion are fairly high.

A good trademark should distinguish the owner's goods or services from those of competitors. The most distinctive trademarks use words that are either "arbitrary" (e.g., Apple® for computers) or "coined" (e.g., Kodak®, Xerox®, or Exxon®) because the likelihood of someone using that word for the same product or service is fairly low. Often, though, marks are selected with words that are "suggestive" (e.g., Dolphin™ for swim wear). Marks that are descriptive (e.g., Superior, Best, EZ) are protectable, if at all, only after considerable use and recognition in the market place. Generic words (e.g., Flexible Catheter™ for a flexible catheter) should be avoided because they cannot function as trademarks and are virtually impossible to federally register and protect as marks, as they fail to identify a unique source of the goods or services represented by the mark.

The selection and protection of trademarks and company names is a sophisticated area and the entrepreneur should consult with a patent or trademark attorney experienced in that specialty before making a choice. Most entrepreneurs will want to increase awareness of their businesses and products online, and the selection of an Internet domain name involves many of the same issues encountered with trademarks.

Protecting Other Intellectual Property

Reasonable steps should be taken to protect all of the intellectual property of any new start-up. Books, manuals, posters, computer programs, works of art, audio and video recordings, and other creative works should be protected under the copyright laws, but note that computer programs may also qualify for patent protection. Make sure that all officers and employees of a company have signed employment agreements with nondisclosure provisions. Trade secrets such as a customer list, sensitive drawings, and the like should be labeled "confidential" and safely stored. Sensitive areas of a plant should be guarded and visitors to high-tech locations should be made to sign a logbook. All of these steps will help a new company retain its rights to its intellectual property.

Afterword

The two major reasons that entrepreneurs often receive little or nothing from their inventions are inexperience and poor marketing—not the lack of inventiveness. A successful entrepreneur must work hard and expect setbacks. Success is typically the result of the inventor working together with a network of capable people experienced in marketing, accounting, law, technology, sales, and related skills. It is extremely rare for an entrepreneur to move an invention successfully into the marketplace without substantial outside help. Even if all of the factors are in place, the public may turn down an Edsel. But the chance for success is there. Others have achieved it—remember the Polaroid® camera and the Xerox® photocopying machine.

Good Luck!

APPENDIX A
ADDRESSES OF THE U.S. PATENT AND TRADEMARK OFFICE AND PROFESSIONAL INTELLECTUAL PROPERTY ORGANIZATIONS

Organizations which provide information and publications of interest to inventors and which should be consulted first:

The United States Patent Office maintains a website providing resources for independent inventors at http://www.uspto.gov/web/offices/com/iip/index.htm.

Using the index and search of the USPTO home website, basic as well as detailed information about patents, trademarks, and copyrights can be obtained, as well as access to databases, manuals, lists of patent attorneys and patent agents by state, forms, copies of patents, etc.

The USPTO can be also contacted by mail or telephone at:
U.S. Patent and Trademark Office
Washington, D.C. 20231
8000-PTO-9199 or 800-786-9199
(571) 272-1000

The Government Printing Office has an online bookstore and a catalog of government publications. It can be reached at:
e-mail: ContactCenter@gpo.gov
http://www.access.gpo.gov/

The American Bar Association, Section of Intellectual Property Law maintains a website and provides online sale publications of interest to inventors:
http://www.abanet.org/intelprop/home.html

Publications:
"What is a Patent?" Second Edition—# 5370157–$12.00
"What is a Trademark?" Second Edition—# 5370156–$12.00
"What is a Copyright?" Second Edition—# 5370155–$12.00

American Intellectual Property Law Association
241 18th Street South, Suite 700
Arlington, VA 22202 (703) 415-0780 Fax: (7030) 415-0786
http://www.aipla.org/

Publications:
"How to Protect and Benefit from your Ideas"—$20.00
"What Is a Patent, Copyright, Trademark"

Other Resources
The Lemelson-MIT program's Invention Dimension
    http://web.mit.edu/invent/invent-main.html
The Patent Cafe
    http://www.patentcafe.com/
Intellectual Property Owners Association
    http://www.ipo.org/
Inventors' Digest Online
    http://www.inventorsdigest.com/
Federal Trade Commission
    http://www.ftc.gov/
Inventors Assistance League
    http://www.inventions.org/
From Patent to Profit
    http://www.frompatenttoprofit.com/index.htm
Inventor Resources by InventorEd. Inc
    http://www.InventorEd.org/inv-reso/

APPENDIX B
REFERENCE COLLECTIONS OF U.S. PATENTS AVAILABLE FOR PUBLIC USE IN PATENT DEPOSITORY LIBRARIES

Current information about depository libraries can be obtained from the USPTO website http://www.uspto.gov/web/offices/com/sol/og/.

Information current as of April 17, 2007:

The following libraries, designated as Patent and Trademark Depository Libraries (PTDLs), provide public access to patent and trademark information received from the United States Patent and Trademark Office (USPTO). This information includes all issued patents, all registered trademarks, the Official Gazette of the U.S. Patent and Trademark Office, search tools such as the Cassis CD-ROM suite of products, and supplemental information in a variety of formats including online, optical disc, microfilm, and paper. Each PTDL also offers access to USPTO resources on the Internet and to PubWEST (Web based examiner search tool), a system used by patent examiners that is not available on the Internet.

Staff assistance and training are provided in the use of this information. All information is available free of charge. However, there may be charges associated with the use of photocopying and related services. Hours of service to the public vary, and anyone contemplating use of these collections at a particular library is urged to contact that library in advance about its services and hours to avoid inconvenience.

State	Name of Library	Telephone Contact
Alabama	Auburn University Libraries	(334) 844-1737
	Birmingham Public Library	(205) 226-3620
Alaska	Anchorage: Z. J. Loussac Public Library	(907) 562-7323
California	Los Angeles Public Library	(213) 228-7220
	Sacramento: California State Library	(916) 654-0069
	San Diego Public Library	(619) 236-5813
	San Francisco Public Library	(415) 557-4500

California *(continued)*	Sunnyvale Public Library	(408) 730-7300
	Riverside: University of California, Riverside Libraries	(951) 827-3226
Colorado	Denver Public Library	(720) 865-1711
Delaware	Newark: University of Delaware Library	(302) 831-2965
Dist. of Columbia	Washington: Howard University Libraries	(202) 806-7252
Florida	Fort Lauderdale: Broward County Main Library	(954) 357-7444
	Miami-Dade Public Library	(305) 375-2665
	Orlando: University of Central Florida Libraries	(407) 823-2562
Georgia	Atlanta: Price Gilbert Memorial Library, Georgia Institute of Technology	(404) 894-1395
Hawaii	Honolulu: Hawaii State Public Library System	(808) 586-3477
Idaho	Moscow: University of Idaho Library	(208) 885-6235
Illinois	Chicago Public Library	(312) 747-4450
	Springfield: Illinois State Library	(217) 782-5659
Indiana	Indianapolis-Marion County Public Library	(317) 269-1741
	West Lafayette Siegesmund Engineering Library, Purdue University	(765) 494-2872
Iowa	Des Moines: State Library of Iowa	(515) 242-6541
Kansas	Wichita: Ablah Library, Wichita State University	1 (800) 572-8368
Kentucky	Louisville Free Public Library	(502) 574-1611
Louisiana	Baton Rouge: Troy H. Middleton Library, Louisiana State University	(225) 388-8875

Maine	Orono: Raymond H. Fogler Library, University of Maine	(207) 581-1678
Maryland	Baltimore: University of Baltimore Law Library	(410) 837-4554
	College Park: Engineering and Physical Sciences Library, University of Maryland	(301) 405-9157
Massachusetts	Amherst: Physical Sciences Library, University of Massachusetts	(413) 545-2765
	Boston Public Library	(617) 536-5400 Ext. 4256
Michigan	Ann Arbor: Media Union Library, University of Michigan	(734) 647-5735
	Big Rapids: Abigail S. Timme Library, Ferris State University	(231) 592-3602
	Detroit: Public Library	(313) 833-1450
Minnesota	Minneapolis Public Library and Information Center	(612) 630-6000
Mississippi	Jackson: Mississippi Library Commission	(601) 961-4111
Missouri	Kansas City: Linda Hall Library	(816) 363-4600 Ext. 724
	St. Louis Public Library	(314) 241-2288 Ext. 390
Montana	Butte: Montana College of Mineral Science and Technology Library	(406) 496-4281
Nebraska	Lincoln: Engineering Library, University of Nebraska—Lincoln	(402) 472-3411
Nevada	Las Vegas—Clark County Library District	(702) 507-3421
	Reno: University of Nevada, Reno Library	(775) 784-6500 Ext. 257
New Jersey	Newark Public Library	(973) 733-7779
	Piscataway: Library of Science and Medicine, Rutgers University	(732) 445-2895
New Mexico	Albuquerque: University of New Mexico General Library	(505) 277-4412

New York	Albany: New York State Library	(518) 474-5355
	Buffalo and Erie County Public Library	(716) 858-7101
	Rochester Public Library	(716) 428-8110
	New York Library (The Research Libraries)	(212) 592-7000
	Stony Brook: Engineering Library, State University of New York	(631) 632-7148
North Carolina	Charlotte	(704) 687-2241
	Raleigh: D.H. Hill Library, North Carolina State University	(919) 515-2935
North Dakota	Grand Forks: Chester Fritz Library, University of North Dakota	(701) 777-4888
Ohio	Akron—Summit County Public Library	(330) 643-9075
	Cincinnati and Hamilton County, Public Library of	(513) 369-6932
	Cleveland Public Library	(216) 623-2870
	Columbus: Ohio State University Libraries	(614) 292-3022
	Dayton: Paul Laurence Dunbar Library, Wright State University	(937) 775-3521
	Toledo/Lucas County Public Library	(419) 259-5209
Oklahoma	Stillwater: Oklahoma State University Center for International Trade Development	(405) 744-7086
Oregon	Portland: Paul L. Boley Law Library, Lewis & Clark College	(503) 768-6786
Pennsylvania	Philadelphia, The Free Library of	(215) 686-5331
	Pittsburgh, Carnegie Library of	(412) 622-3138
	University Park: Pattee Library, Pennsylvania State University	(814) 865-7617
Puerto Rico	Mayaquez General Library, University of Puerto Rico	(787) 993-0000 Ext. 3244
	Bayamon, Learning Resources Center, University of Puerto Rico	(787) 786-5225

Rhode Island	Providence Public Library	(401) 455-8027
South Carolina	Clemson University Libraries	(864) 656-3024
South Dakota	Rapid City: Devereaux Library, South Dakota School of Mines and Technology	(605) 394-1275
Tennessee	Nashville: Stevenson Science Library, Vanderbilt University	(615) 322-2717
Texas	Austin: McKinney Engineering Library, University of Texas at Austin	(512) 495-4500
	College Station: West Campus Library, Texas A & M University	(979) 845-2111
	Dallas Public Library	(214) 670-1468
	Houston: The Fondren Library, Rice University	(713) 348-5483
	Lubbock: Texas Tech University	(806) 742-2282
	San Antonio Public Library	(210) 207-2500
Utah	Salt Lake City: Marriott Library, University of Utah	(801) 581-8394
Vermont	Burlington: Bailey/Howe Library, University of Vermont	(802) 656-2542
Virginia	Richmond: James Branch Cabell Library, Virginia Commonwealth University	(804) 828-1101
Washington	Seattle: Engineering Library, University of Washington	(206) 543-0740
West Virginia	Morgantown: Evansdale Library, West Virginia University	(304) 293-4695 Ext. 5113
Wisconsin	Madison: Kurt F. Wendt Library, University of Wisconsin Madison	(608) 262-6845
	Milwaukee Public Library	(414) 286-3051
Wyoming	Cheyenne: Wyoming State Library	(307) 777-7281

Appendix C
Inventor Organizations

A wealth of useful information is available on the Internet and can be accessed by using a search engine, but the inventor should be careful to discriminate genuinely helpful vs. exploitative websites.

A partial list of mainly national organizations follows:

United Inventors Association
999 Lehigh Station Road
Henrietta, NY 14467-9311
Tel: (585) 359-9310
Fax: (585) 359-1132
E-mail: UIAUSA@aol.com
http://www.uiausa.com

National Congress of Inventor Organizations (NCIO)
P.O. Box 931881
Los Angeles, CA 90093-1881
Tel: 323 878-6952
E-mail: ncio@inventionconvention.com
http://www.inventionconvention.com/ncio

American Society of Inventors
P.O. Box 58426
Philadelphia, PA 19102
Tel: (215) 546-6601
E-mail: info@asoi.org

Invention Place
Tel: (888) 54-INPEX (US & Canada only)
Or (412) 288-2136
Fax: (412) 288-1343
E-mail: info@inventionshow.com
http://www.inventionplace.com/

Appendix D
Indices of Manufacturing Companies Found in Many Public Libraries and on the Web

The Thomas Register
http://www.thomasnet.com/

Standard and Poor's Register

D & B Business Ranking

Million Dollar Directory

Department of Commerce
http://www.doc.gov/

APPENDIX E
SOURCES OF FINANCIAL ASSISTANCE

The following website provides a list of invention and small business resource funding:

U.S. Small Business Administration:
   http://www.sba.gov

Small Business Innovation Research Program (SBIR)
   http://www.sba.gov/sbir/indexsbir-sttr.html
SBIR is a highly competitive program that encourages small business to explore their technological potential and provides the incentive to profit from its commercialization.

Small Business Investment Companies Program (SBIC)
   http://www.sba.gov/INV/

U.S. Department of Energy, Office of Industrial Technology
   http://www1.eere.energy.gov/industry/

The Ben Franklin Technology Partners
   http://www.benfranklin.org/

For local sources of funding the state-by-state resources should be consulted (see Appendix C).

About the ABA Section of Intellectual Property Law

From its strength within the American Bar Association, the ABA Section of Intellectual Property Law (ABA-IPL) advances the development and improvement of intellectual property laws and their fair and just administration. The Section furthers the goals of its members by sharing knowledge and balanced insight on the full spectrum of intellectual property law and practice, including patents, trademarks, copyright, industrial design, literary and artistic works, scientific works, and innovation. Providing a forum for rich perspectives and reasoned commentary, ABA-IPL serves as the ABA voice of intellectual property law within the profession, before policy makers, and with the public.